Communication Dilemma

Terms and Conditions

LEGAL NOTICE

Table Of Contents

Foreword

People often don't really understand or fully grasp the merits of good communication, and this has been a point of contention for these same people. Being able to communicate not only effectively but also within the right context is something that should be thoroughly understood if one intends to make and grow a successful business. Get all the info you need here.

Communication Crunch
Secrets To Successful Communication For Sales

Chapter 1:

Communication Basics

Synopsis

The following are some contributing factors that good communication will highlight:

The Basics

Acquiring and keeping a good workforce or strong staff base is very important to any business endeavor whether it is small or big.

Therefore in the quest to keep all parties happy and functioning the key is to practice good communication always. Good communication allows the smooth flow of information to be divulged and accepted by all parties thus creating a clear picture of what is expected and desired.

Without communication there is the real possibility of encountering problems simply because everyone is doing what they think is best thus not coordinating and working as a team. The results of this are usually unpleasant and definitely not positive.

Good communication skill will also help to establish the individual in the business arena, thus creating the platform for respect and authority in the particular venture.

This will also help to ensure customers will be more than willing to generate return sales due to the effective communication expounded.

Communication does not only mean divulging information, it also means having a keen listening ear. This is a highly prized element for customers and is definitely well received, when the tone of the communication clearly shows the business owner understands the customers' needs.

Good communication also ensures fewer mistakes are made and this is also another important fact to be conscious of. Not considering its importance, could eventually lead to costly mistakes, some of which are not easy to recover from.

Chapter 2:

Synopsis

For people intending to venture into the business arena, even if it is through the online platform where there is usually very minimal or at the very least some level of control exercised, there is a very real need to have some level of self esteem firmly in place.

Self

Self esteem is a very dominant element that dictates the general perception formed by outsiders, towards the business owner and the business content being touted.

If the individual lacks the amount of self esteem needed to make an impressive impact on the client or customer base, then there is a very real chance that a positive outcome from the encounter will not be achieved. This could eventually adversely affect the future of the business endeavor altogether.

The following are some points to consider when trying addressing the self esteem issue:

Paying attention to the outward presentation of an individual is one of the forefront issues that should be addressed. It is unfortunate, yet very true, when people say first impressions count.

There is nothing more off putting that to be in a situation where the presenter is not appropriately representing the business entity. Both in presentation material and in the person itself, there should be a semblance of professionalism.

Being confident or practicing to appear confident at all times, is a tool that every business person should make the effort of fine tune.

People who are confident are better able to tackle or be perceived to tackle any situation that present itself. When confidence if clearly displayed there will actually be very little resistance or opposition to what is being presented and the chances of actually making a sale is definitely much higher.

Confidence is usually something that is acquired through time and experience. Therefore the business owner should be more willing to try new and innovative ways of getting people interested in the business at hand.

Chapter 3:

Oral Communication Strategies

Synopsis

Oral communication skills are often linked to business successes and this fact has long been one that most people understand and acknowledge. Small and large business entities understand the importance of good oral communications and thus seek to improve this skill whenever possible.

The Talk

There following points will further emphasize the merits of having good and effective oral communication skills:

Presentations are often the first medium used during initial encounters with potential clients and customers. With good oral communication skills, the presenter is able to present the intended material in a clear and convincing manner thus giving the aura of professionalism.

This professionalism perception will adequately ensure little or no opposition is voiced in regard to the presented material simply due to the fact most listeners would be convinced and enticed by the presenter's confident oral communication skills.

Oral communication is also a dominant factor needed in the client interaction phase. This crucial stage basically cements any possible future that the business has with the other party.

If the interaction goes well and the client is convinced and happy, the main contributing factor would be the part played by the oral communication.

Oral communication also needed within the inter office interaction for the offline and online business entity alike. This encompasses the various levels of information that needs to be communicated for the purpose of running the business smoothly.

Although there are some defining perimeters such as the various levels of personnel involved, oral communication is still seen as the most effective medium of passing and receiving information.

Oral communication also provides the more personal connection to the information being presented. With the other electronically styled information dispensing there is no real connective feeling that can be measure other than the choice of words put into the written material.

Chapter 4:

Synopsis

Written communication techniques are something that all business owners should make an effort to master or equip themselves with. Communicating through this medium is commonly used and cannot be sidelined in favor of other options.

Understanding the effectiveness of written communication will encourage the business owner to ensure every written communication is well prepared and effective in its content form.

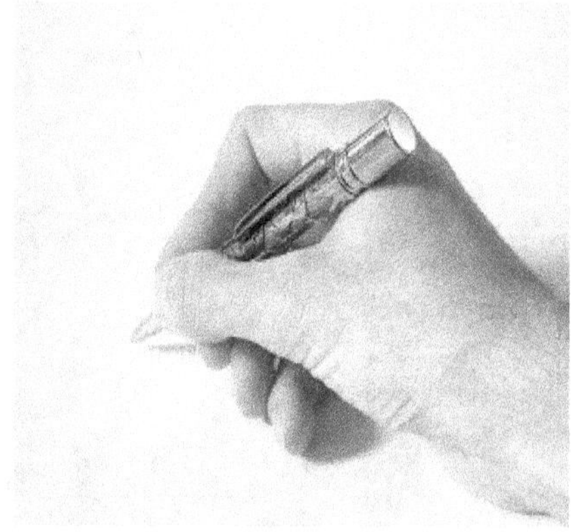

Writing

The following are some of the advantages of acquiring good written communication skills:

The element of clarity is depicted in a written form of communication and this is often used in very serious scenarios as legal binding entities.

Written communication helps to lay down the clear requirements and principals the parties are agreeing upon, thus paving the way for smoother running of the organizational engine.

Written communication also provides the means to make something fairly permanent in nature, which is useful for documenting and maintaining records.

In the business arena, this is an important tool to fall back on, as a reference point or for its clarification value.

This form of communication also helps to create the proper delegation of responsibilities in a clear and undisputed style, as everything is documented and available for immediate reference.

It also conveniently eliminates the possibility of miscommunication and misunderstandings, although these two elements may still sometimes be found but rarely so.

Because of the way the information is presented, there is an element of definition, precision and explicitness, therefore the enhancement of the organization's image is well perceived and preserved.

Form a legal point of view, there are very few other platforms that can provide undisputed information that is acceptable as a defining factor in a possible dispute.

All business entities should make it a point to keep any form of communication backed up in written style to ensure negative elements do not jeopardize the business at any given time.

Chapter 5:

Synopsis

Body language is second only to the power of the spoken word but nonetheless just as impacting. With this in mind it is important for those venturing into the business arena be well aware of how they are presenting themselves.

The Body

The following are some points to be aware of when trying to make an impression:

Standing – the position of the back should be straight as possible while keeping the shoulders straight and the head in an upright position.

This position is meant to give the impression of being firm and confident. It also means the individual is very comfortable and at ease both with himself or herself and with the surroundings.

Sitting – keeping a sitting position that is complimenting to the individual is important as no one want to be privy to any personal effects.

Sitting up right at all time also gives the impression of being alert and ready to be actively involved in the situation at hand. Sitting quietly also is important as any movement will be perceived as being nervous or uncomfortable.

Hands – although most people tend to wave or move their hands about when talking this should not be encouraged especially in a more formal setting.

The usual connection would be the more excited the tone of the conversation the more animated the hand movements would be, therefore there is a need to consciously observe and correct this before anyone becomes embarrassed.

Head movement – nodding at appropriate intervals to show acknowledgment or agreement is acceptable as long as it is not overdone.

Bobbing the head too much would then cause the individual to become a joke, and so, not taken seriously.

Facial expressions – this is the most telling of all body movement as it immediately informs the other party of the individual's thoughts. Learning to control the facial expressions is a very important and needed trait to exercise.

Chapter 6:

Public Speaking Tips

Synopsis

Most people in the business at some point or another will be in a situation where public speaking is part of the promotional exercise of the business connection. Public speaking is not necessarily directed to just a large audience, as it can also be addressed to a smaller group of people. The idea behind the public speaking exercise is to be able to present information in an interesting and informative way.

In Public

The following are some tips as to what an individual attempting to engage in a public speaking exercise should focus on:

Public speaking requires a certain level of conviction to be incorporated into the general delivery of the material being presented.

This aura of conviction is the element that is going to connect with the receiving party to create the interest in the material being presented.

Besides the interest element, a presentation given with conviction will also encourage the listener to be more convinced and this effectively ensures the conversion to loyal customer bases.

Public speaking is more effective if done without having to read from prepared notes. Besides the probability of the material read out being less than engaging, there is also the danger of not being able to connect with the audience as the presenter is too busy reading the said material.

Maintaining eye contact is perhaps one of the more important elements to pay attention to and ensure that it is constantly practiced.

Without the ever important eye contact there is little chance of the presenter being able to hold the attention of the audience for long.

Even with exciting material being presented the eye contact element is necessary as it also gives the presenter a chance to gauge the receptiveness of the audience towards the material being presented.

This would help the presenter make the necessary on the spot adjustments to ensure the negative effect is not continuous.

Chapter 7:

How Bad Communication Damages Your Business

Synopsis

Regardless of the size of the business endeavor, bad communications can have a very negative impact on the said business and sometimes the impact is so detrimental that the eventual results may be almost impossible to correct. Therefore it is important to acknowledge that bad communication should be curbed or even eliminated at all costs.

Some Tips

The following are some areas that can be affected by bad communications:

A company's production levels can be severely affected by the use of bad communications, as this leads to a breakdown in communications and also productivity. When this happens, goals and deadlines are usually jeopardized.

Bad communications, can also lead to poor morale among the workers, which will also eventually spill over into the general business platform. Not understanding what is expected, thus performing below expectations will contribute to a lot of confusion and stagnation within the company's processes, which in turn will negatively impact the daily progress anticipated.

Mistakes are very common because of poor or bad communication skills of those issuing orders. In some cases this makes the already existing bad communications become even worse as the blaming exercise commences. Therefore it is very important to ensure all connected to a particular exercise understand all that is expected.

If poor communication still abound then there should be some form of readdress that can be encouraged to help overcome any negativity.

Wrapping Up

Bad communication also contributes negatively to the overall progress of the business as little headway is made in terms of sales and visibility of the business, product or service being offered. Bad communication can also create misunderstandings that can be costly. Rejection of products because they fail to meet the standards of the customer, is not an unusual phenomenon when bad communication is rife.

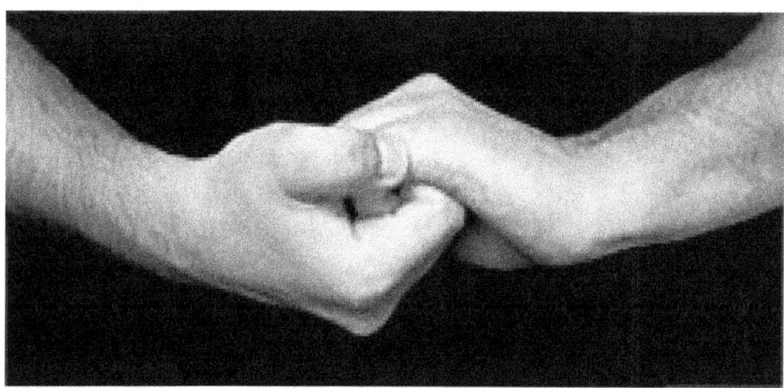